Biggest, Baddest Books

BIGGEST, BADDEST BOOK OF
STORMS

MARY ELIZABETH SALZMANN

Consulting Editor, Diane Craig, M.A./Reading Specialist

Super Sandcastle

An Imprint of Abdo Publishing
www.abdopublishing.com

www.abdopublishing.com

Published by Abdo Publishing, a division of ABDO, PO Box 398166, Minneapolis, Minnesota 55439. Copyright © 2015 by Abdo Consulting Group, Inc. International copyrights reserved in all countries. No part of this book may be reproduced in any form without written permission from the publisher. Super SandCastle™ is a trademark and logo of Abdo Publishing.

Printed in the United States of America, North Mankato, Minnesota
102014
012015

Editor: Liz Salzmann
Content Developer: Nancy Tuminelly
Cover and Interior Design and Production: Mighty Media, Inc.
Photo Credits: Shutterstock, NOAA, TIME-LIFE

Library of Congress Cataloging-in-Publication Data

Salzmann, Mary Elizabeth, 1968-
 Biggest, baddest book of storms / Mary Elizabeth Salzmann.
    pages cm -- (Biggest, baddest books)
 Audience: 004-009.
 ISBN 978-1-62403-519-7
1. Storms--Juvenile literature. I. Title. II. Series: Biggest, baddest books.
 QC941.3.S25 2015
 551.55--dc23
                2014024007

Super SandCastle™ books are created by a team of professional educators, reading specialists, and content developers around five essential components—phonemic awareness, phonics, vocabulary, text comprehension, and fluency—to assist young readers as they develop reading skills and strategies and increase their general knowledge. All books are written, reviewed, and leveled for guided reading, early reading intervention, and Accelerated Reader® programs for use in shared, guided, and independent reading and writing activities to support a balanced approach to literacy instruction.

CONTENTS

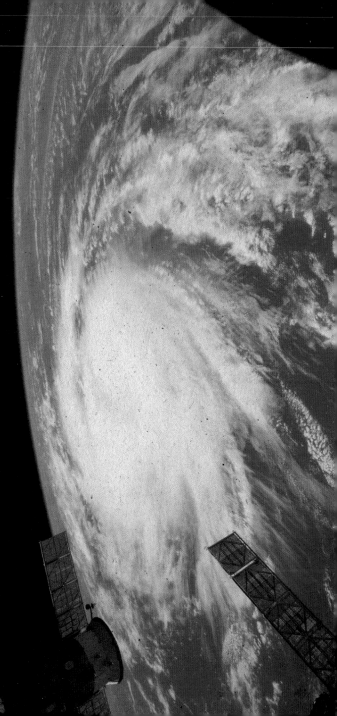

WHAT IS A STORM?

A storm starts in the atmosphere. What happens there affects things on the ground. Storms bring wind, lightning, rain, hail, and snow.

HIGH PRESSURE

LOW PRESSURE

HIGH PRESSURE VS. LOW PRESSURE

The atmosphere is the air that surrounds the Earth. The air presses on the Earth. An area where the air presses harder is a high-pressure area. An area where the air presses less hard is a low-pressure area.

BIRTH of a STORM

The air pressure is always changing. Sometimes a high-pressure area forms around a low-pressure area. They push against each other. It gets windy. Clouds appear. This is how a storm begins.

Some storms are very strong. A strong storm can be **dangerous**. It can destroy buildings and kill people.

STORM TYPES

There are different kinds of storms. The kind of storm depends on where it is. It also depends on the season.

BLIZZARD

DUST STORM

FIRESTORM

HAILSTORM

ICE STORM

SNOWSTORM

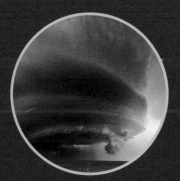

THUNDERSTORM

TORNADO

TROPICAL CYCLONE

TERRIFYING TWISTERS

Tornadoes can form when there are storm clouds. They happen when it is very windy and the air is wet. The wind lifts the **moist** air up to a cloud. It spins it around. This makes a **column** of spinning air. Sometimes it touches the ground. Then it can blow buildings down. It can also carry things away.

TORNADO FACTS

- The wind in a tornado blows 40 to 300 miles per hour (64 to 483 kmh).

- Not all tornadoes touch the ground. If they do, it's usually just for a short **distance**. But some stay on the ground for many miles.

- A tornado can be more than 1 mile (1.6 km) wide. Most are much smaller.

A HOME DAMAGED BY A TORNADO

WEDNESDAY, MARCH 18, 1925

No 2.

TRI-STATE TERROR

The strongest single tornado was the Tri-State Tornado. It happened on March 18, 1925. It passed through Missouri, Illinois, and Indiana. The total **distance** was 219 miles (352 km). It moved 73 miles per hour (117 kmh). It killed 695 people.

THE TORNADO'S DEVASTATION IN GRIFFIN, INDIANA

2011 SUPER OUTBREAK

Many tornadoes at once are called a tornado outbreak. There was a super outbreak on April 25th through 28th, 2011. There were 358 tornadoes. They happened in 21 U.S. states and southern Canada. This outbreak caused 324 deaths. Most were in Alabama.

SATELLITE VIEW OF THE STORM ON APRIL 27, 2011

SMITHVILLE, MISSISSIPPI

PHIL CAMPBELL, ALABAMA

CORDOVA, ALABAMA

RINGGOLD, GEORGIA

FURY FROM THE SEA

Sometimes a low-pressure area rotates over a warm ocean. This can cause strong winds. It can also produce a lot of rain. This is a tropical cyclone.

The wind can reach 74 miles per hour (119 kmh). Then the storm is called a hurricane, typhoon, or cyclone.

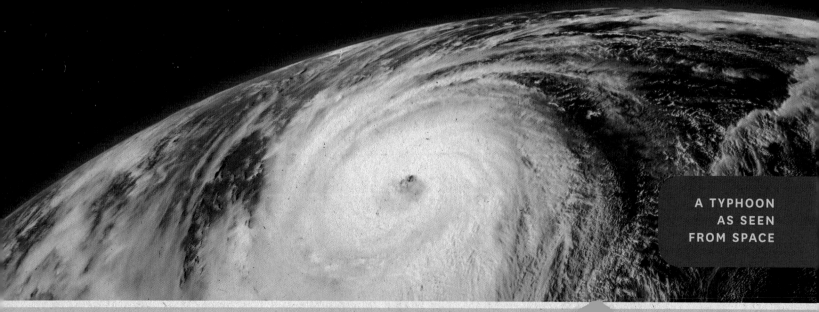

A TYPHOON AS SEEN FROM SPACE

STORM SURGE

Strong winds over an ocean can cause a storm surge. The wind presses on the surface of the ocean. This causes the water to rise. The storm blows the high wall of water. If it hits land, it causes flooding. A storm surge is often the most **dangerous** part of a storm.

What's in a Name?

Hurricane, typhoon, and cyclone are all the same thing. The name used depends on where it happens.

- *Hurricanes are in the North Atlantic Ocean, Caribbean Sea, Gulf of Mexico, or the eastern North Pacific Ocean.*

- *Typhoons are in the western North Pacific Ocean.*

- *Cyclones are in the Indian Ocean.*

90 MPH (145 KMH) WINDS CAUSE HUGE WAVES

SAVAGE CYCLONES

GALVESTON HURRICANE

This hurricane happened on September 8, 1900. It was the deadliest natural **disaster** in the United States. About 8,000 people died. The whole island of Galveston flooded. Nearly every building was destroyed.

Hurricane Katrina

This hurricane happend in August 2005. It flooded many areas along the coast. The worst hit places were Louisiana and Mississippi. About 2,000 people died.

Hurricane Sandy

This hurricane happened in 2012. It killed about 300 people. It started in the Caribbean Sea. It reached the United States on October 29th. It caused a lot of **damage** in New York and New Jersey.

Typhoon Haiyan

This typhoon happened on November 7, 2013. It struck the Philippines. The wind blew 195 miles per hour (315 kmh). That's the strongest wind of any storm to reach land. Several thousand people died. Nearly 2 million people were left homeless.

SNOWED IN

Places with cold winters have snowstorms. Snow is pretty. It sparkles. It makes things look clean. It's fun to play in. But too much snow can be **dangerous**.

FORECAST: BLIZZARD

The worst winter storms are blizzards. Three things make a blizzard.

1. It's cold! Below 20 degrees Fahrenheit (–7 C).

2. Strong winds! At least 35 miles per hour (56 kmh).

3. It snows a lot! Or the wind blows snow around. It is hard to see where you are going.

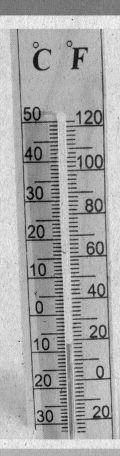

COLD

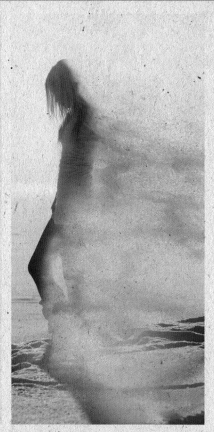

WINDY

SNOWY

WORST. WINTER. EVER.

The winter of 1888 was one of the deadliest. Two of the worst blizzards ever happened that year.

THE SCHOOLHOUSE BLIZZARD

This storm occurred on January 12th and 13th. It happened in the Great Plains. It suddenly got very cold. It was −37 degrees **Fahrenheit** (−38 C). It got very windy. Snow started falling fast.

Some schools closed early. The children were sent home. But many of them didn't make it. More than 200 people died in this blizzard. Most of them were children.

Huge snowdrifts in Springfield, Massachusetts

THE GREAT BLIZZARD

The Great Blizzard of 1888 happened on March 11th and 12th. More than 400 people died.

It was in the northeastern United States. They got 20 to 60 inches (51 to 152 cm) of snow. It buried houses and trains. People were trapped in their houses.

The wind blew more than 45 miles per hour (72 kmh). It caused 200 ships to sink.

A snow-covered ship in Lewes Harbor, Delaware

Snow on the Brooklyn Bridge, New York City (March 14, 1888)

ICE STORMS

Ice storms can also happen in winter. They occur when it rains and the water **freezes**. This makes a layer of ice. If it is ¼ inch (.6 cm) thick, it is an ice storm.

Ice is heavy. It can cause power lines and trees to fall down. The ice also covers streets. Cars slide off the road.

There was a bad ice storm in Idaho in January 1961. It created the thickest layer of ice ever recorded. It was 8 inches (20 cm) thick.

DUST STORMS

Dust storms happen where there is dry dirt or sand. The wind picks up dust. It blows it around. The flying dust can be **dangerous**. A dust storm makes it hard to see. It can create a wall of dust 1 mile (1.6 km) high.

Dust storms **damage** crops. They blow the good soil away. They can also hurt growing plants.

There was a big dust storm in Arizona. It happened on July 5, 2011. The wind blew more than 60 miles per hour (97 kmh). Dust from the desert blew into Phoenix.

FIRESTORMS

A fire needs air to burn. It pulls air into itself. The more air it draws in, the stronger it grows. It creates strong winds. The winds keep the fire burning.

Firestorms are more likely if it is already windy. Or if the wind suddenly increases. This can start a firestorm. Or it can make one worse. Earthquakes, bombs, and other explosions can also cause firestorms.

THE PESHTIGO FIRESTORM

There was a deadly firestorm on October 8, 1871. It happened near Peshtigo, Wisconsin. It created a huge wall of flame. It was 1 mile (1.6 km) high and 5 miles (8 km) wide. It destroyed 12 towns. Between 1,200 and 2,500 people died.

WHAT DO YOU KNOW ABOUT STORMS?

1. ALL TORNADOS TOUCH THE GROUND. **TRUE OR FALSE?**

2. A STORM SURGE IS OFTEN THE MOST **DANGEROUS** PART OF A STORM. **TRUE OR FALSE?**

3. A BLIZZARD IS A WARM, WINDY STORM. **TRUE OR FALSE?**

4. A DUST STORM CAN CREATE A DUST WALL 1 MILE (1.6 KM) HIGH. **TRUE OR FALSE?**

ANSWERS: 1) FALSE 2) TRUE 3) FALSE 4) TRUE

GLOSSARY

COLUMN – a narrow pillar.

DANGEROUS – able or likely to cause harm or injury.

DAMAGE – to cause harm or hurt to someone or something.

DEVASTATE – to destroy much or most of something.

DISASTER – a sudden event that causes destruction and suffering or loss of life.

DISTANCE – the amount of space between two places.

FAHRENHEIT – a scale used to measure temperature in the U.S. customary system.

FREEZE – to become solid ice from being in the cold.

MOIST – slightly wet.